ISSUES
today

Hu ssues

Edited

Series Ed

ol.115

Independence Educational Publishers

Acknowledgements

The publisher is grateful for permission to reproduce the material in this book. While every care has been taken to trace and acknowledge copyright, the publisher tenders its apology for any accidental infringement or where copyright has proved untraceable. The publisher would be pleased to come to a suitable arrangement in any such case with the rightful owner.

Illustrations

All illustrations, including the front cover, are by Don Hatcher.

Images

All images courtesy of iStock, except: page 5 © Ira Gelb.

Icons on pages 9 and 23 are made by Freepik from www.flaticon. com.

Editorial by Christina Hughes and layout by Jackie Staines, on behalf of Independence Educational Publishers.

Printed in Great Britain by Zenith Print Group.

Cara Acred

Cambridge

September 2016

Contents

About *ISSUES* today

ISSUES today is a series of resource books on contemporary social issues, designed for Key Stage 3 pupils and above. This series is also suitable for Scottish P7, S1 and S2 students.

Each volume contains information from a variety of sources, including government reports and statistics, newspaper and magazine articles, surveys and polls, academic research and literature from charities and lobby groups. The information has been tailored to an 11 to 14 age group; it has been rewritten and presented in a simple, straightforward and accessible format.

In addition, each **ISSUES** today title features handy tasks and assignments based on the information contained in the book, for use in class, for homework or as a revision aid.

ISSUES today can be used as a learning resource in a variety of Key Stage 3 subjects, including English, Science, History, Geography, PSHE, Citizenship, Sex and Relationships Education and Religious Education.

About this book

Human Rights Issues is Volume 115 in the **ISSUES today** series.

Shockingly, 46% of children are unaware of their own human rights. From the Human Rights Act to the European Convention on Human Rights, this book addresses what human rights are and the debate surrounding them: Is Internet access a human right? Should prisoners have the right to vote? What would be the effect on human rights if the UK leaves the EU? This book also covers human trafficking, child marriage and the teaching of equality and human rights.

Human Rights Issues offers a useful overview of the many issues involved in this topic. However, at the end of each article is a URL for the relevant organisation's website, which can be visited by pupils who want to carry out further research.

Because the information in this book is gathered from a number of different sources, pupils should think about the origin of the text and critically evaluate the information that is presented. Does the source have a particular bias or agenda? Are you being presented with facts or opinions? Do you agree with the writer?

At the end of each chapter there are two pages of activities relating to the articles and issues raised in that chapter. The 'Brainstorm' questions can be done as a group or individually after reading the articles. This should prompt some ideas and lead on to further activities. Some suggestions for such activities are given under the headings 'Oral', 'Moral dilemmas', 'Research', 'Written' and 'Design' that follow the 'Brainstorm' questions.

For more information about **ISSUES** today and its sister series, **ISSUES** (for pupils aged 14 to 18), please visit the Independence website.

www.independence.co.uk

What are human rights?

Human rights belong to every member of the human family regardless of sex, race, nationality, socio-economic group, political opinion, sexual orientation or any other status.

Human rights are universal. They apply to all people simply on the basis of being human.

Human rights cannot be taken away from someone. They cannot be taken away simply because we do not like the person seeking to exercise their rights. They can only be limited in certain tightly-defined circumstances and some rights, such as the prohibition on torture and slavery, can never be limited.

Human rights are indivisible. This means you cannot pick and choose which rights you want to honour. Many rights depend on each other to be meaningful – so, for example, the right to fair trial would be meaningless without the prohibition on discrimination, and the right to free speech must go hand in hand with the right to assemble peacefully.

Human rights are owed by the State to the people – this means public bodies must respect your human rights and the Government must ensure there are laws in place so that other people respect your human rights too. For example, the right to life requires not only that the actions of those working on behalf of the State do not lead to your death, but that laws are also in place to protect you from the actions of others that might want to do you harm.

Human rights were first recognised internationally by the Universal Declaration on Human Rights in 1948. This was quickly followed by the adoption, two years later, of the European Convention on Human Rights. In 1998 the Human Rights Act was passed, making the rights and freedoms in the European Convention on Human Rights directly enforceable in the UK. It entered into force on 2 October 2000.

The UK is also a party to a number of other international instruments that seek to protect and promote other human rights.

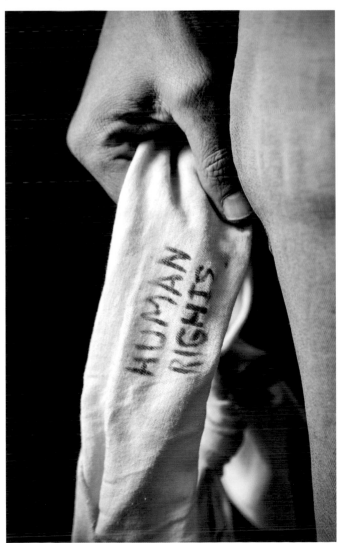

International human rights

The Universal Declaration of Human Rights

In 1948, in the aftermath of the Second World War, the newly formed United Nations adopted the Universal Declaration of Human Rights (UDHR). In response to the horrible acts committed before and during the War, the international community sought to define the rights and freedoms necessary to secure the dignity and worth of each individual.

The European Convention on Human Rights and the Council of Europe

In Europe, another newly formed international body, the Council of Europe, set about giving effect to the UDHR in a European context. The resulting European Convention on Human Rights was signed in 1950 and ratified by the United Kingdom, one of the first countries to do so, in 1951.

At the time there were only ten members of the Council of Europe (the countries subscribed to the Convention), and all were Western European. The Council has since expanded, particularly following the collapse of the communist states in Eastern Europe. Now 47 member countries subscribe to the European Convention.

Over the years a number of additional Protocols to the Convention have been adopted. Only some of these grant new rights. The United Kingdom has ratified some but not all of these substantive Protocols.

Other international human rights instruments

Over the years, a number of other international human instruments giving effect to the UDHR have been drafted and adopted. Some of these are truly international, e.g. the International Covenant on Civil and Political Rights, while others are regional, e.g. the American Convention on Human Rights and the African Charter on Human and Peoples' Rights. Some deal with specific issues, e.g. the Convention against Torture, and some with the rights of specific groups, e.g. the Refugee Convention and the Convention on the Rights of the Child. The United Kingdom has ratified many of these international conventions.

The European Court of Human Rights and enforcement of the European Convention

The European Convention system was unusual in that, very early on, a court was set up to interpret and ensure compliance with the Convention. The European Court of Human Rights was established in 1959 and the United Kingdom has allowed an individual right of application to the Court since 1966. Before applying to the Court, applicants are required to pursue any legal proceedings in this country that are capable of giving them redress for the violation of their Convention rights. Now that the Human Rights Act is in force, this will usually involve pursuing a claim under the Act.

Enforcement of other international instruments

The example of a regional human rights court has been followed under both the Inter-American and African systems. Other international human rights systems have established committees to which complaints of breaches can be made, provided the relevant government allows. Apart from the European Convention, the only international human rights instrument under which the United Kingdom permits an individual right of complaint is the Convention on the Elimination of all Forms of Discrimination against Women (CEDAW).

Some international instruments require participating states to report regularly on what they are doing to ensure compliance. Groups such as Liberty often participate in these reporting cycles by commenting on their government's report, or by producing a shadow report.

International human rights instruments in British law

The Human Rights Act was passed in 1998 in order to 'give further effect' to the European Convention in British law. Under the Act, public authorities in this country are now required to act in a way that respects people's rights under the Convention, and people can now rely on their Convention rights in legal proceedings.

This is not the case with the other international human rights instruments that the United Kingdom has ratified. While people can refer to these in proceedings before the British courts, the courts will not directly apply them. They may still have some effect for two reasons:

➢ Where there is some ambiguity as to what the law requires, the courts will assume that the law should be interpreted in a way that complies with the United Kingdom's international obligations;

➢ In interpreting the rights under the European Convention, the courts here, but more particularly the European Court of Human Rights, will have regard to other international human rights instruments.

www.liberty-human-rights.org.uk

Mini glossary

Compliance – *if you comply with something this means that you agree to follow that request or condition.*

Prohibition – *the act of banning or forbidding something.*

Ratified – *to approve of something and come to an agreement.*

Redress – *to right a wrong.*

What is human trafficking?

Human trafficking involves recruiting, transporting or holding a person by use of threats, coercion or deception in order to exploit them. Essentially, it is the oppression and abuse of people motivated by financial or personal gain. It is often described as a form of modern day slavery.

Trafficking happens all over the world, across international borders and within countries. In the UK each year about 2,000 men, women and children are helped to escape from trafficking, but this is just the tip of the iceberg. The Government estimates there are 10,000 – 13,000 victims of modern slavery in the UK.

Victims of trafficking are often tricked into coming to the UK by false promises or because of threats against them or their family. People are trafficked into prostitution, pornography, agricultural and building labour, manufacturing, domestic servitude, forced begging, benefit fraud, petty criminality and organ removal. They are forced to work for little or no pay; they may have limited freedom and poor living conditions. Many experience physical or emotional abuse.

> Mary fled her village in Nigeria because of abuse from the community elders. Whilst living on the streets of the capital city she met a man called Tony who told her she could get a good job in England. He bought her a ticket and came with her to London. Hours after she arrived, Mary was taken to a brothel where she was locked in a room. For many months she was forced to have sex with up to ten or 12 men a day who paid money to Tony.

What is CARE doing?

CARE has been working to address human trafficking since 2006. We raise awareness and work for changes in the law and Government polices across the UK Parliaments and Assemblies.

We were actively involved in the development of new laws across the UK in 2015, supporting amendments to the Modern Slavery Act 2015 and the Human Trafficking and Exploitation (Scotland) Act 2015. We also acted as the principal advisor to Lord Morrow, who took the Human Trafficking and Exploitation (Criminal Justice and Support for Victims) Act (Northern Ireland) 2015 through the Assembly. However, there is still more to be done.

Our work focuses on these areas:

➢ tackling the demand for human trafficking for sexual exploitation

➢ ensuring that survivors of exploitation are given adequate care and protection

➢ provision of special support for child victims

➢ strong action against those who exploit others.

How can I respond?

You can stay informed about what the Government is doing by signing up to our Loose the Chains e-mails: care.org.uk/loosethechains-signup.

You can write to your MP and your MSPs, AMs or MLAs or arrange to meet them in person, either alone or with other supporters. Our Loose the Chains e-mails will highlight specific opportunities to do so.

You can contact your Police and Crime Commissioner (in England and Wales) to encourage them to make trafficking a key priority in your area.

You can speak about this issue to people that you know. Contact your local newspaper, or speak at your church, school or student groups. You can join with people in your area to campaign together.

You can be watchful for signs of trafficking and keep your eyes open for it in your community. Understand the signs at: modernslavery.co.uk.

If you suspect an instance of trafficking in your area you can contact:

➢ the Police (101 or 999 if someone is in immediate danger)

➢ Crimestoppers (0800 555 111 or crimestoppers-uk.org) where you can leave information anonymously.

Do not confront a suspected trafficker or victim of trafficking. Your safety and that of any possible victims is of primary importance.

You can pray for survivors and those continuing to experience exploitation, for police and for politicians as they work to prevent and reduce human trafficking.

You can find more ideas of how to take action and further information on this issue at: care.org.uk/humantrafficking

April 2016

www.care.org.uk

Types of human trafficking

There are several broad categories of exploitation linked to human trafficking:

Sexual exploitation

Sexual exploitation involves any non-consensual or abusive sexual acts performed without a victim's permission. This includes prostitution, escort work and pornography. Women, men and children of both sexes can be victims. Many will have been deceived with promises of a better life and then controlled through violence and abuse.

Forced labour

Forced labour involves victims being made to work very long hours, often in hard conditions and to hand over almost all of their wages to their traffickers. Forced labour usually means use of pressure and lack of freedom or choice for the victim. In many cases, victims are threatened verbally and physically to make them do things.

Manufacturing, entertainment, travel, farming and construction industries have been found to use forced labour by victims of human trafficking to some extent. There has been a marked increase in reported numbers in recent years. Often large numbers of people are housed in single dwellings and there is evidence of 'hot bunking', where a returning shift takes up the sleeping accommodation of those starting the next shift.

The International Labour Organization (ILO) has identified six elements which can suggest forced labour. These are:

➢ Threats or actual physical harm

➢ Being made to stay at the workplace or to a limited area

➢ Debt-bondage

➢ Not paying wages or keeping hold of a large portion of wages that go against previously made agreements

➢ Taking away and keeping hold of passports and identity documents (the workers can leave or prove their identity status)

➢ If a worker is there illegally they will threaten to tell the authorities.

Domestic servitude

Domestic servitude involves the victim being forced to work in private households. Their movement will often be restricted and they will be forced to perform household tasks such as child care and house-keeping over long hours and for little if any pay. Victims will lead very isolated lives and have little or no unsupervised freedom. Their own privacy and comfort will be minimal, often sleeping on a mattress on the floor in an open part of the house.

In rare circumstances where victims receive a wage, it will be heavily reduced, as they are charged for food and accommodation.

Organ harvesting

Organ harvesting involves trafficking people in order to use their internal organs for transplant. The illegal trade is dominated by kidneys, which are in the greatest demand. These are the only major organs that can be wholly transplanted with relatively few risks to the life of the donor.

Child trafficking

Children are particularly vulnerable to exploitation by individual traffickers and organised crime groups. They can be deliberately targeted by crime groups, or ruthlessly exploited by the people who should protect them. About a quarter of the victims referred to the UK Human Trafficking Centre are children.

Common countries of origin include Vietnam, Nigeria, Romania, Slovakia and the UK.

www.nationalcrimeagency.gov.uk

Common myths about human trafficking

1. Human trafficking and people smuggling are the same thing

There are important differences between human trafficking and people smuggling. The main difference is the element of exploitation. People being smuggled as illegal migrants have usually consented to being smuggled. Trafficking victims have not consented, or have been tricked into consent.

What happens to each of them at the end of their journey will also be very different. The relationship between an illegal migrant and a people smuggler is a commercial transaction which ends on completion of the journey. However, for people who are trafficked, the purpose of the journey is to put them somewhere where they can be exploited for the sake of the traffickers' profits. The journey is only the beginning.

It can be difficult to tell the difference between trafficking and smuggling scenarios for many reasons, including:

➢ People who begin as smuggled migrants may become victims of trafficking, i.e. there is a change of circumstances at some point during the process

➢ The same people acting as traffickers may also act as smugglers and use the same routes for both trafficking and smuggling

➢ Conditions for smuggled persons may be so bad that it is difficult to believe that they consented to it.

2. You cannot be a victim of trafficking if you gave your consent to be moved

Someone becomes a victim of trafficking not because of the journey they make but because of the exploitation they experience at the end of that journey.

Any consent they give to make the journey in the first place is likely to have been gained through trickery, for example with the promise of a job or a better standard of living and this turns out to be a lie.

This is why the Palermo Protocol makes clear that human trafficking is about the three elements of movement, control and exploitation.

3. Trafficking only affects people from other countries

Whilst people smuggling always involves illegal border crossing and entry into another country, human trafficking for exploitation can happen within someone's own country, including Britain.

4. Many trafficked women are already prostitutes

This is a common misconception. The majority of trafficking victims working as prostitutes will have been forced into it against their will. They have often been trafficked without their consent, deceived into consenting to the journey or deceived about the kind of work they would be doing at the end of the journey.

The above information is reprinted with kind permission from the National Crime Agency. © Crown copyright 2016

www.nationalcrimeagency.gov.uk

Mini glossary

Consent – giving permission to do something.

Exploitation – being taken advantage of.

Palermo Protocol – three protocols put in place by the United Nations to help prevent, suppress and punish traffickings in persons, especially women and children.

European Convention on Human Rights

The European Convention on Human Rights (ECHR) is an international human rights treaty, which means an agreement between governments. It gives all people – adults, children and young people – a set of rights, such as the right to life and the right to freedom of religion.

The ECHR is divided into 'articles', or sections. Each article contains a different right. You can read about these below.

The Human Rights Act 1998 made the ECHR part of domestic law, which means that a person can take their case to court in England if they think their rights have been breached. If the English courts reject their claim, they can then take it to the European Court of Human Rights.

The rights in the ECHR are:

Article 1: To have your human rights respected by the state.

Article 2: The right to life.

Article 3: Freedom from torture and inhuman or degrading treatment or punishment.

Article 4: Freedom from slavery.

Article 5: Right to liberty and security.

Article 6: The right to a fair trial, including the child's right to be informed promptly, in a language he or she understands, of the alleged offence and to have an interpreter in court if he or she cannot understand or speak the language used in court. Restrictions on reporting can be applied to protect the interests of children.

Article 7: No one can be punished for an act that was not a criminal offence when it was carried out.

Article 8: The right to respect for private and family life, home and correspondence.

Article 9: The right to freedom of thought, conscience and religion.

Article 10: The right to freedom of expression.

Article 11: The right to freedom of assembly and association.

Article 12: Right to marry.

Article 13: Right to an effective remedy.

Plus Article 2 of the First Protocol (a later addition) – the right to education, which must conform with parents' religious and philosophical convictions.

These are all supported by Article 14, which says that all the rights in the Convention apply to all people without discrimination.

Articles 8 to 11 are qualified rights – they can be interfered with, but only for a good reason (like public safety, economic wellbeing or the protection of the rights of others), in accordance with the law generally and only so far as is necessary in the individual case.

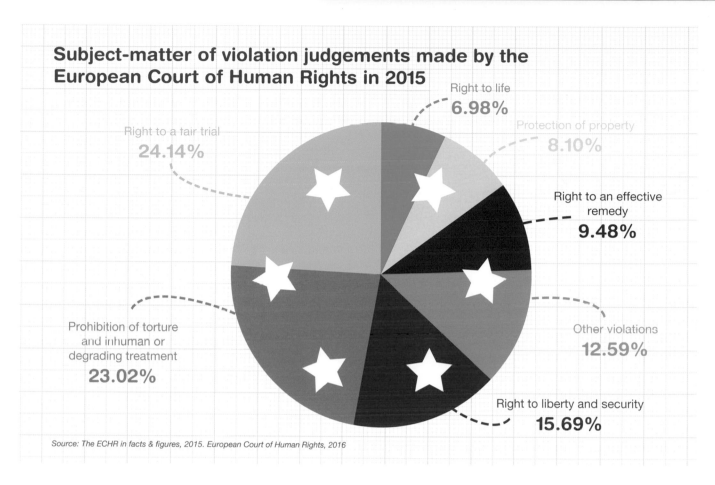

Subject-matter of violation judgements made by the European Court of Human Rights in 2015

Right to life
6.98%

Protection of property
8.10%

Right to a fair trial
24.14%

Right to an effective remedy
9.48%

Prohibition of torture and inhuman or degrading treatment
23.02%

Other violations
12.59%

Right to liberty and security
15.69%

Source: The ECHR in facts & figures, 2015. European Court of Human Rights, 2016

Children's rights

When the UK courts are considering a claim by a child under the Human Rights Act, they should refer to the UN Convention on the Rights of the Child which the UK Government ratified in 1991.

"It further protects children's rights by setting standards in health care, education and legal, civil and social services."

The Grand Chamber of the European Court of Human Rights has stated that:

The human rights of children and the standards to which all governments must aspire in realising these rights for all children are set out in The Convention on the Rights of the Child... The Convention spells out the basic human rights that children everywhere – without discrimination – have: the right to survival; to develop to the fullest; to protection from harmful influences, abuse and exploitation; and to participate fully in family, cultural and social life. It further protects children's rights by setting standards in health care, education

and legal, civil and social services. States party to The Convention are duty-bound to develop and undertake all actions and policies in the light of the best interests of the child (Article 3). Moreover, States have to ensure that a child is not separated from his or her parents against their will unless such separation is necessary for the best interests of the child, and respect the right of a child who is separated from one or both parents to maintain personal relations and direct contact with both parents on a regular basis, except if it is contrary to the child's best interests (Article 9) (Sahın v Germany 2003).

www.crae.org.uk

Human rights and the EU

What would be the effect on human rights if the UK leaves the EU?

By Joshua Rozenberg

Some things won't change – and some things will.

We would still be signed up to the European Convention on Human Rights

The United Kingdom has signed the European Convention on Human Rights, which is an international treaty enforced by the Council of Europe – a group of 47 countries from Iceland to Russia.

As a result, people who believe that the UK government or the UK's laws are responsible for a breach of any of the rights listed in the convention can challenge them at the European Court of Human Rights in Strasbourg.

By signing the treaty, the government agreed to abide by any judgement delivered by the Strasbourg court that goes against the UK. To comply, the government might have to ask parliament to change the law.

It's the job of the Council of Europe to supervise the way in which governments give effect to the court's rulings.

The Council of Europe is entirely separate from the European Union, which has 28 members.

It follows that a country can be a member of the Council of Europe and not of the EU. And while ministers say that they "rule nothing out", it is not the policy of the UK government to leave the Council of Europe or pull out of the Human Rights Convention.

So if the UK leaves the EU it will still be possible for people to complain to the Human Rights Court and it will still be the responsibility of the UK to abide by the court's judgements.

The Human Rights Act is also separate from the EU

From 1966 to 2000, the only way in which an individual could enforce the European Convention on Human Rights against the government was to complain to the court in Strasbourg.

But when the Human Rights Act was brought into force, courts in the United Kingdom were required to give effect to other laws in a way that was compatible with human rights.

The act also required courts in the UK to take into account decisions by the human rights court in Strasbourg.

That won't change if the UK leaves the EU. There will be no obligation on parliament to change the Human Rights Act – although that's something that the government is separately committed to.

The EU court's role in human rights

So far, we have been talking about the Council of Europe's human rights court in Strasbourg.

But the European Union has its own, entirely separate, court system in Luxembourg. Its formal title is the Court of Justice of the European Union (CJEU) but it's also known as European Court of Justice.

The main job of the CJEU is to interpret EU law and make sure it's applied in the same way in all EU countries.

The Court of Justice has a judge from each EU member country. As the top court of the EU, it can give judgements about the legality of EU action and the compatibility of national action with EU law. There is also another EU court, the General Court, which has specialist responsibilities.

Another important role is to decide legal disputes between EU institutions and member governments.

In 2000 the EU adopted a Charter of Fundamental Rights. This became legally binding in December 2009, when the Treaty of Lisbon came into force.

The charter is consistent with the human rights convention. Where the rights in the charter "correspond to" the rights in the human rights convention, their meaning is the same.

But EU law may give greater protection than the Council of Europe convention. The charter also includes additional rights that are not in the convention, relating to areas such as social policy, data protection and bioethics.

The charter is addressed to the EU institutions "with due regard for the principle of subsidiarity".

And the charter's provisions are also binding on EU states, but only when those states are using EU law – which means giving effect to a provision of EU law.

There may also be limits on using some of the charter's contents in court, as some provisions are intended to guide to EU lawmakers and decision-makers rather than judges.

Wasn't the UK supposed to get an opt-out from EU human rights laws?

Unlike human rights law, EU law is directly binding on the courts of the United Kingdom. It takes priority over other laws.

So when the charter was given effect by parliament, some people in the UK were concerned that its provisions could be used to overturn existing laws.

To address these concerns, the government negotiated an additional section to the Treaty of Lisbon, known as Protocol 30.

This says, in part: "The charter does not extend the ability of the CJEU, or any court or tribunal of... the United Kingdom, to find that the laws, regulations or administrative provisions, practices or action of... the

United Kingdom are inconsistent with the fundamental rights, freedoms and principles that it reaffirms."

The key word here is 'extend'. Protocol 30 makes it clear that the charter does not give the courts new powers. But it does not limit their existing powers.

National courts and EU courts have long had the power to assess EU-related national laws against existing EU fundamental rights. For this reason, leading lawyers suggested in March 2011 that protocol 30 might have little practical effect.

It was certainly not the 'opt-out' that some people had hoped for.

That view was confirmed by a ruling from the CJEU in December 2011.

Holding that EU states could not return asylum-seekers to countries where they might face inhuman treatment, the court said that Protocol 30 did not exempt a UK court from compliance with the charter. This was something the government had already accepted.

The EU human rights charter has been increasingly used by the courts

Last year, the Court of Appeal 'disapplied' part of a statute giving immunity to foreign embassies and said the charter would allow former embassy staff to sue for unfair dismissal under EU law. Nobody even mentioned Protocol 30.

If the UK were to leave the EU, parliament would be expected to repeal the legislation giving effect to the EU treaties.

As a result, claimants would no longer be able to enforce their EU law rights, including the charter, in the courts of the UK. But they would still be able to rely on the other human rights convention in the ways discussed earlier.

The EU courts are making increasing use of the charter. It was mentioned in 43 judgements in 2011 and 210 judgements in 2014.

If a country is thought to have violated charter rights when using EU law, the European Commission can launch infringement proceedings against the state and, ultimately, take that state to the CJEU.

During 2014, the European Commission brought 11 cases to the CJEU alleging that member states had infringed the charter. Five of those cases relate to asylum and migration.

When a country is found to be at fault in infringement proceedings, it must put things right at once or risk a second case being brought. That may result in a fine.

If the UK were to leave the EU, it would no longer face proceedings for infringing the EU charter. But it would still be bound by its obligations under the non-EU human rights convention.

Leaving the human rights convention without leaving the EU

The Home Secretary has suggested that the UK should stay in the EU but drop out of the separate Council of Europe human rights convention.

Others, whether they like the idea or not, claim that this is impossible because EU members have to be signed up to the human rights convention.

That is the case in practice for countries that want to join the EU as new members, but there isn't a hard and fast rule for existing members.

Legal opinion is divided about whether any of the countries currently in the EU could pull out of the convention and remain in the EU.

24 May 2016

www.fullfact.org

Mini glossary

Alleging – *to state or claim something.*

Binding – *if something is binding it has to be followed and cannot be broken.*

Infringement/infringed – *to break an agreement or law.*

Subsidiarity – *if an individual can do it then society should not take over, or if a small society can do it, larger societies should not take over.*

How Human Rights Law helps all sorts of people get justice

By Jack Sommers

As they press ahead with plans to abolish Britain's Human Rights Act (HRA), the Conservatives have been showing people who have benefited from it as villains.

In its much-derided document outlining its plans to abolish the HRA, the party hinted that the current arrangement could see prisoners granted the right to vote over the government's objections and said the HRA empowered "foreign nationals who have committed very serious crimes... to justify remaining in the UK".

Home Secretary Theresa May told her party's 2011 conference: "We all know the stories about the Human Rights Act. The violent drug dealer who cannot be sent home because his daughter – for whom he pays no maintenance – lives here.

"The robber who cannot be removed because he has a girlfriend. The illegal immigrant who cannot be deported because... he has a pet cat."

The HRA itself does not give us its rights, including to the one to "family life" May was so frustrated by.

They come from the European Convention on Human Rights (ECHR), written and ratified in the 1950s, whose guarantees to certain rights the HRA introduced to British courts.

After the long fight to deport Abu Qatada, May said withdrawing from the ECHR altogether should be an option.

In their document published last year, the Tories said they would have "no alternative" but to withdraw from the ECHR if the Council of Europe refused to recognise any new Bill of Rights as legitimate.

But anyone who thinks abolishing the HRA and withdrawing from the ECHR would only mean prisoners could not vote and foreign-born criminals would be easier to deport is wrong.

Here are some of the groups of people who won fights for justice thanks to the ECHR, either by going to court in Strasbourg or, thanks to the HRA, in Britain.

Families of missing people

The "right to family life" has become the villain of the HRA for how it complicates deporting those born abroad when convicted of crimes here. But this part of became crucial in the ongoing hunt for Ben Needham, who disappeared in 1991 when he was just 21 months old.

Barrister Ian Brownhill, who has acted for the Needham family, the mother of Ben Needham for free, told HuffPost UK that this right granted by the act was "essential" in his advocacy.

He wrote to the Home Office asking why it had taken ten months to reply to a funding request from South Yorkshire Police, after which it gave the force £700,000 to pay for English detectives to travel to Greece to continue the search.

Brownhill said: "'In over 20 years since Ben Needham went missing the family never had a lawyer. They had no idea what Ben's rights or theirs' were. Last year I volunteered to help fill that gap.

"The Needhams' right to a family life has been part of the successful campaign to persuade the government to fund a new investigation into Ben's disappearance. It's an honour and a pleasure as a lawyer to help the Needhams' understand and exercise their human rights."

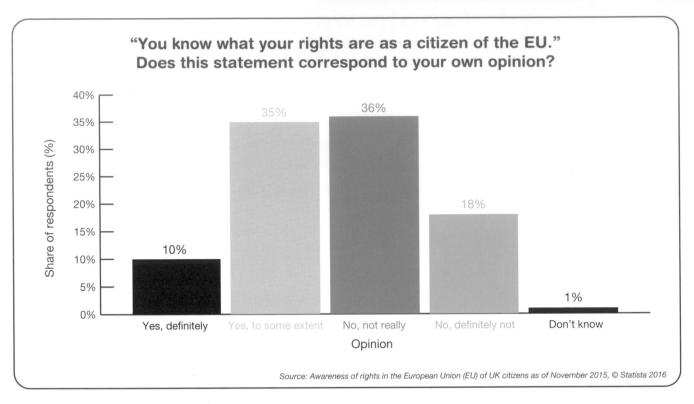

"You know what your rights are as a citizen of the EU."
Does this statement correspond to your own opinion?

Source: Awareness of rights in the European Union (EU) of UK citizens as of November 2015, © Statista 2016

Rape victims failed by the police

Two victims of cab driver rapist John Worboys received damages after winning their claim that the Metropolitan Police breached their human rights when it botched an investigation that left him free to keep attacking.

The women argued, and The High Court agreed, that the forces' repeated failings to catch him breached their article 3 right to be spared inhuman or degrading treatment.

Mr Justice Green said one of the women would not have been raped but for "myriad failings in the investigative process".

Worboys, who was jailed in 2009, is believed to have attacked more than 100 women.

Gay people kicked out of the military

Four people brought a case that ended the military's ban on gay people serving that forced them to leave the armed forces.

Duncan Lustig-Prean, Jeannette Smith, Graeme Grady and John Beckett said the ban breached their right to privacy – granted under the European Convention on Human Rights. The European Court on Human Rights in Strasbourg ruled in their favour in September 1999.

Three months after the judgement, the ban on gay people in the military was lifted. Then-defence secretary Geoff Hoon told the Commons sexuality was "essentially a private matter for the individual".

Victims of human trafficking

A Tanzanian woman was 'tricked' into coming to the UK in 2006 by the woman she worked for. She ended up being forced to work long hours for her parents as an unpaid domestic servant. She was fed only stale food, forced to sleep on a mattress on the kitchen floor and only allowed out to attend church on Sundays.

She fled their home – only to be forced to work in another home and fell very ill, developing a major breathing problem that would require lung surgery and Post-Traumatic Stress Disorder.

In 2010, the Home Office ordered she be sent back to Tanzania. Using the ECHR's ban on "forced labour", her lawyer successfully argued the British state owed her – time to recover from the ordeal – for its failure to protect her from being trafficked into and then within the UK.

A tribunal held that, in light of this, demanding she leave the UK, where she was being treated, would be 'unreasonable'.

The grieving families of dead soldiers

A new inquest into the death of a soldier at Deepcut Barracks was ordered after a threat of litigation under the Human Rights Act by civil rights campaigners Liberty.

Private Cheryl James was one of four soldiers to be found dead from gunshot wounds at the Surrey barracks. The original inquest in 1995 lasted only an hour and failed to speak to key witnesses or review important evidence, Liberty claimed.

Last year, a new inquest was ordered. Lawyers for the family had obtained 44 volumes of statements, documents, notes and photographs after threatening litigation under the Human Rights Act.

Her parents Doreen and Des James said: "Something went dreadfully wrong at Deepcut yet until now no one has bothered to look at how and why our daughter died. We can only hope that Cheryl's legacy helps change the current ineffective and discredited military justice system."

The new inquest will look whether a third party was involved in her death and what happened on the evening before she died.

Disabled people

The Supreme Court found that three people had been deprived of their liberty by virtue of the restrictions imposed upon them by authorities caring for them.

Two sisters, who both had learning difficulties, and a man born with cerebral palsy were living in a foster home, a residential home and a social services-arranged accommodation respectively – under close supervision to support them. One of the sisters was sometimes physically restrained when she was not co-operative.

Lower courts ruled the trio's treatment did not amount to a deprivation of liberty, which meant the living arrangements need not be subject to independent checks to ensure it was still in their best interests.

The Supreme Court noted that the European Court of Human Rights had made it clear it was "important not to confuse the question of the benevolent justification for the care arrangements with the concept of deprivation of liberty. Human rights have a universal character and physical liberty is the same for everyone, regardless of their disabilities".

Children

A nine-year-old boy was repeatedly beaten by his stepfather with a cane. The case went to trial with the man accused of assault occasioning actual bodily harm. A doctor had examined the boy and found him covered in bruises.

The judge told the jury: "This case is not about whether you should punish a very difficult boy. It is about whether what was done here was reasonable or not and you must judge that." They declared the stepfather not guilty.

The case reached the European Court on Human Rights in 1998 (again, this was before the HRA made going to British court an option). It found the law, which allowed parents to hit their children provided it was "reasonable chastisement", had failed to protect the child and breached his right to not suffer inhumane treatment. In 2004, parliament changed the "reasonable chastisement" defence so that it did not apply in such serious assaults.

27 May 2015

www.huffingtonpost.co.uk

Mini glossary

Abolish – to put an end to something. To cancel or wipe it out.

Advocacy – a legal advocate is someone who argues someone's case.

Benevolent – kind.

Chastisement – to punish.

Deport – to force someone to leave the country, usually for having committed a crime.

Inquest – a formal investigation into something that has happened.

Litigation – taking legal action.

Myriad – a great number of things.

Ratified – to approve of something and come to an agreement.

Tribunal – a special committee to help solve disagreements.

Activities

Brainstorm

1.   What is the Human Rights Act?

2.   What is human trafficking?

3.   What is the Palermo Protocol?

Oral activity

4.   Choose an article from the *European Convention on Human Rights* on page 6 and, in pairs or small groups, discuss how your life might change if this right was taken away.

Research activity

5.   Research the UN Convention on the Rights of the Child and write a short summary of what it is.

Written activities

6.   In pairs, create a PowerPoint presentation that explores the indicators of human trafficking. Include a section that advises people what they should do if they suspect someone has been 'trafficked'.

7.   Create an informative booklet to explain what the Human Rights Act 1998 is.

Moral dilemma

8.   'Britain's Human Rights Act (HRA) should be abolished.' Discuss this statement as a class.

Design activities

9.   In small groups, design a campaign that will highlight the issue of forced labour. Your campaign could take electronic, video or printed form. Include samples of your campaign material and a written plan of at least 500 words explaining your thinking behind the campaign.

10. Design a poster that highlights one particular type of human trafficking (e.g. child trafficking, forced labour, etc.).

Analysis: which human rights matter most?

New data from seven countries in Europe plus the USA reveals the importance different cultures place on different rights around the world.

By Peter Kellner

This is what we did. We identified thirty rights that appear in United Nations and European Council declarations, in the British and American Bills of Rights and, in some cases, are the subject of more recent debate in one or more countries. To prevent the list being even longer, we have been selective. For example, we have omitted 'the right of subjects to petition the king', and the right of people not to be punished prior to conviction, which were promised by Britain's Bill of Rights. Matters requiring urgent attention in one era are taken for granted in another.

Even so, thirty is a large number. So we divided the list into two, and asked people to look at each list in turn, selecting up to five of the 15 rights from each list that 'you think are the most important'. This means that respondents could select, in all, up to ten rights from the thirty. This does not mean that people necessarily oppose the remaining rights, simply that they consider them less important than the ones they do select.

This is what we found:

➢ The right to vote comes top in five of the eight countries (Britain, France, Sweden, Finland and Norway), and second in two (Denmark and the United States – in both cases behind free speech). Only in Germany does it come lower, behind free speech, privacy, free school education, low-cost health care and the right to a fair trial.

➢ In all eight countries more than 50% select free speech as one of the most important rights. It is the only right to which this applies.

➢ Views vary about the importance of *habeas corpus* – the right to remain free unless charged with a criminal offence and brought swiftly towards the courts. It is valued most in Denmark (by 49%) and the United States (40%). In Britain, where *habeas corpus* originated in the seventeenth century, the figure is just 27%.

➢ Rights to free school education and low-cost health care are selected by majorities in six of the eight countries. The exceptions are France and the United States. In the US,

Ranking rights around the world: top five most important rights in each country

Numbers show the percentage of adults in each country who say each right is most important out of a choice of five.

Britain
1. Vote (66%)
2. Fair trial if charged (61%)
3. Free or low-cost healthcare (61%)
4. Roam without fear of attack (60%)
5. Free school education for children (57%)

USA
1. Free speech (69%)
2. Privacy (63%)
3. Vote (61%)
4. Fair trial if charged (60%)
5. Pursue a religion of choice (53%)

Germany
1. Free speech (66%)
2. Privacy (57%)
3. Free school education for children (52%)
4. Fair trial if charged (50%)
5. Free or low-cost healthcare (50%)

France
1. Vote (54%)
2. Free speech (52%)
3. Basic pension for older people (50%)
4. Minimum wage at work (48%)
5. Roam without fear of attack (45%)

Denmark
1. Free speech (72%)
2. Vote (71%)
3. Free or low-cost healthcare (67%)
4. Fair trial if charged (67%)
5. Free school education for children (57%)

Sweden
1. Vote (72%)
2. Free speech (71%)
3. Roam without fear of attack (58%)
4. Free or low-cost healthcare (56%)
5. Free school education for children (55%)

Finland
1. Vote (63%)
2. Roam without fear of attack (60%)
3. Free speech (58%)
4. Free or low-cost healthcare (57%)
5. Free school education for children (55%)

Norway
1. Vote (64%)
2. Free school education for children (60%)
3. Free or low-cost healthcare (60%)
4. Live free from discrimination (59%)
5. Free speech (51%)

In all eight countries **more than 50% select free speech** as one of the most important rights. It is the only right to which this applies.

Source: *Analysis: which human rights matter most?*, YouGov, 30 March 2016

this reflects a different history and culture of public service provision. In France, unlike the other six European countries we surveyed, financial rights (to a minimum wage and a basic pension) come higher than the rights to health and education.

➢ France is out of line in three other respects. It has by some margin the lowest figure for the right to live free from discrimination – and the highest figures for the right to a job and the 'right to take part with others in anti-government demonstrations'.

➢ Few will be surprised that far more Americans than Europeans value the right to own a gun (selected by 46% of Americans, but by no more than 6% in any European country) and 'the right of an unborn child to life' (30%, compared with 13% in Germany and no more than 8% in any of the other six countries).

➢ The French and Americans are also keener than anyone else on 'the right to keep as much of one's own income as possible with the lowest possible taxes'. In the case of the United States, this is consistent with limited expectations of public-sector provision of health, education and pensions. With France it's more complex: public services do not rank as high as in the six other European countries, but jobs, pay and pensions matter a lot. In their quest for security, income AND low taxes, many French voters appear to make demands on the state that seem likely to lead to disappointment. Perhaps this, as well as the lingering memory of France's revolutionary past, explains the enthusiasm of so many French voters on both Left and Right to mount anti-government demonstrations.

➢ In Europe, property rights matter less than social rights. In Germany only 6% regard 'the right to own property, either alone or in association with others' as one of their most valued human rights. The figures are slightly higher for France (14%) and Britain (16%) and higher still in the four Scandinavian countries (20-29%). Only in the United States (37%) is it on a par with the rights to free school and low-cost health care.

➢ There are striking differences in views to rights that are matters of more recent controversy. In most of the eight countries, significant numbers of people value 'the right to communicate freely with others' (e.g. by letter, phone or e-mail) without government agencies being able to access what is being said). Four in ten Germans and Scandinavians regard this as one of their most important rights, as do 35% of Americans. But it is valued by rather fewer French (29%) and British (21%) adults.

➢ Much lower numbers choose the right of gay couples to a same-sex marriage: the numbers range from 10% (Finland) to 19% (US). This is a clear example of a reform that, separate YouGov research has found, is now popular, or at least widely accepted – but not considered by most people to be as vital a human right as the others in our list.

➢ In six of the eight countries, many more people value 'the right of women to have an abortion' than 'the right of an unborn child to life'. The exceptions are France, where both rights score just 13%, and the United States, where as many as 30% choose the right of an unborn child to life as a key human right, compared with 21% who value a woman's right to an abortion. The countries with the strongest support for abortion rights are Denmark and Sweden.

Those are the main facts. Each of them deserves a blog, even a book, to themselves. It's not just the similarities and differences between countries that are significant, but the variations between different demographic groups within each country. For example, British men value free speech more than women, while women place a higher priority on the rights to free schooling and low-cost health care.

Nor does this analysis tell us about direct trade-offs. How far are people willing to defend free speech in the face of social media trolls – and *habeas corpus* when the police and security services seek greater powers to fight terrorism? Past YouGov surveys have generally found that, when push comes to shove, most people give security a higher priority than human rights.

The results reported here, then, do not provide a complete map of how human rights are regarded in the eight countries we surveyed. But they do give us a baseline. They tell us what matters most when people are invited to consider a wide range of rights that have been promoted over recent decades and, in some cases, centuries. It is, I believe, the first survey of its kind that has been conducted.

It won't be the last. Understanding public attitudes to human rights, like promoting and defending those rights, is a never-ending task. It is also a vital one, just like giving voters, customers, workers, patients, passengers, parents – indeed all of us in our different guises – a voice in the institutions that affect our lives. This has been the purpose of YouGov for the past fifteen years and will continue to be so.

30 March 2016

www.yougov.co.uk

Child marriage

Every year 15 million girls are married as children, denied their rights to health, education and opportunity and robbed of their childhood. If we do nothing, by 2030 an estimated 16.5 million girls a year will marry as children.

Each year, 15 million girls are married before the age of 18. That is 28 girls every minute – married off too soon, threatening their personal development and wellbeing. With more young people on our planet than ever before, child marriage is a human rights violation that we must end to achieve a fairer future for all.

Child brides are often made powerless, dependent on their husbands and their fundamental rights to health, education and safety are denied. Neither physically nor emotionally ready to become wives and mothers, child brides are at greater risk of experiencing dangerous complications in pregnancy and childbirth, becoming infected with HIV/AIDS and suffering domestic violence. With little access to education and economic opportunities, they and their families are more likely to live in poverty.

Nations also feel the impact: a system that undervalues the contribution of young women limits its own possibilities. In this way, child marriage drains countries of the innovation and potential that would enable them to thrive.

An ongoing problem

Child marriage continues to happen across countries, fuelled by poverty, social and cultural norms. For many families, it is a viewed as an economic need – one less mouth to feed. Long-held beliefs and traditions based on gender inequality mean that becoming a wife and mother is often deemed a daughter's only choice.

Child marriage facts

➢ More than 700 million women alive today were married before their 18th birthday. That is equal to about 10% of the world's population.

➢ If there is no reduction in child marriage, an additional 1.2 billion girls will be married by 2050.

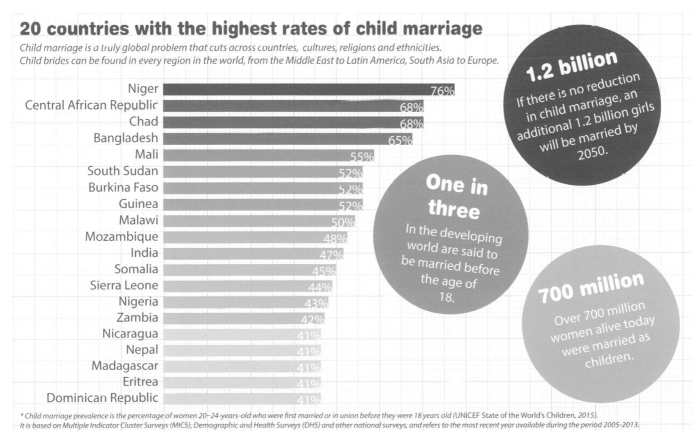

20 countries with the highest rates of child marriage

Child marriage is a truly global problem that cuts across countries, cultures, religions and ethnicities.
Child brides can be found in every region in the world, from the Middle East to Latin America, South Asia to Europe.

Country	Rate
Niger	76%
Central African Republic	68%
Chad	68%
Bangladesh	65%
Mali	55%
South Sudan	52%
Burkina Faso	52%
Guinea	52%
Malawi	50%
Mozambique	48%
India	47%
Somalia	45%
Sierra Leone	44%
Nigeria	43%
Zambia	42%
Nicaragua	41%
Nepal	41%
Madagascar	41%
Eritrea	41%
Dominican Republic	41%

1.2 billion
If there is no reduction in child marriage, an additional 1.2 billion girls will be married by 2050.

One in three
In the developing world are said to be married before the age of 18.

700 million
Over 700 million women alive today were married as children.

* Child marriage prevalence is the percentage of women 20–24-years-old who were first married or in union before they were 18 years old (UNICEF State of the World's Children, 2015).
It is based on Multiple Indicator Cluster Surveys (MICS), Demographic and Health Surveys (DHS) and other national surveys, and refers to the most recent year available during the period 2005-2013.

> ➤ Some child brides are as young as eight or nine.
> ➤ Most adolescent pregnancies (90%) take place within marriage.
> ➤ Pregnancy and childbirth complications are among the leading causes of death in girls aged 15 to 19 in low- and middle-income countries.

Powerful reasons to act now

Globally, the rates of child marriage are slowly declining. Growing commitments to address the issue, such as including the target 5.3 To end child, early and forced marriage in the sustainable development goals, are encouraging. However, there are urgent reasons to double our efforts.

It violates human rights and is illegal

In many countries, child marriage is prohibited, but existing laws are often not enforced or provide exceptions for parental consent or traditional and customary laws. Child marriage reinforces gender inequality and violates human rights. Tolerating any injustice makes it easier for others to exist.

It carries on poverty

Married girls often leave school and so can lack the skills to help lift their families out of poverty. Without addressing child marriage, the international community will fail to achieve its commitment in the sustainable development goals to reduce global poverty.

The longer we wait, the bigger the problem will be

Millions of girls and women already suffer the consequences of child marriage. If we do nothing, population growth means that, by 2050, the total number of women married as children will grow to 1.2 billion, with devastating consequences for girls, their families and their countries. Boys are also affected – 33 million men today were married before the age of 15 and 156 million before the age of 18.

Progress is possible

The complex mix of cultural and economic factors mean there is not a single, simple solution. But, through partnership, long-term programming and a willingness to learn from our successes and failures, we can end child marriage in a generation.

Why does child marriage happen?
Tradition

Child marriage is a traditional practice that in many places happens simply because it has happened for generations – and not following tradition could mean exclusion from the community. But as Graça Machel, widow of Nelson Mandela, says, traditions are made by people – we can change them.

Gender roles

In many communities where child marriage is practised, girls are not valued as much as boys – they are seen as a burden. The challenge will be to change parents' attitudes and emphasise that girls who avoid early marriage and stay in school will likely be able to make a greater contribution to their family and their community in the long term.

Poverty

Where poverty is intense, giving a daughter in marriage allows parents to reduce family expenses by ensuring they have one less person to feed, clothe and educate. In communities where a dowry or 'bride price' is paid, it is often welcome income for poor families; in those where the bride's family pay the groom a dowry, they often have to pay less money if the bride is young and uneducated.

Security

Many parents marry off their daughters young because they feel it is in her best interest, often to ensure her safety in areas where girls are at high risk of physical or sexual assault.

Global pressure

Girls Not Brides shows the will of a global movement to end child marriage. By connecting and broadcasting the voice of civil society organisations across the world, we help instil the global pressure that makes ground-level change happen.

> *The above information is reprinted with kind permission from Girls Not Brides: The Global Partnership to End Child Marriage. © Girls Not Brides 2016*

> **www.girlsnotbrides.org**

> ### Mini glossary
>
> **Dowry** – *money or goods that a bride brings to her husband and his family upon marriage*

Three quarters of Britons consider Internet access a 'human right'

There is overwhelming public support for the idea that access to the Internet should be a human right, according to new research.

By Sophia Curtis

Three quarters of web users in Britain believe affordable access to the Internet should be a basic human right, according to new research.

The study of 23,376 Internet users in 24 countries, commissioned by the Centre for International Governance Innovation (CIGI), revealed that a smaller proportion of Britons regard Internet as a basic human right than the global average (83%).

However, British respondents said the Internet is important for their future in terms of accessing important information and scientific knowledge (90%), personal enjoyment and recreation (91%), social communication (77%), free speech and political expression (79%) and economic future and livelihood (76%).

"Overwhelming global public support for the idea that access to the Internet should be a human right shows just how important the Internet has come to freedom of expression, freedom of association, social communication, the generation of new knowledge and economic opportunity and growth," said Fen Hampson, director of CIGI's Global Security & Politics Program.

"Right now, one third of the world's population is online but two-thirds of the world's population is not. Unless they are brought online, a world of Internet 'have and have-nots' will not only contribute to income inequality, but also stifle the world's full potential for prosperity and innovation."

The news comes after US President Barack Obama urged the communications regulator (FCC) to make equal Internet access a basic right for all Americans

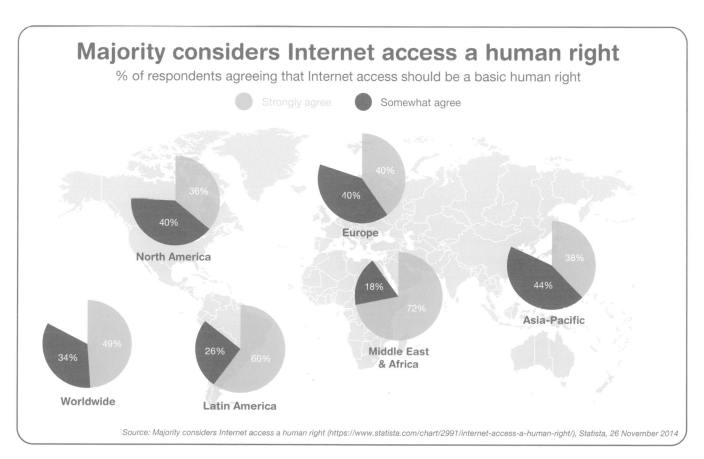

Majority considers Internet access a human right

% of respondents agreeing that Internet access should be a basic human right

● Strongly agree ● Somewhat agree

North America — 36% / 40%

Europe — 40% / 40%

Worldwide — 49% / 34%

Latin America — 60% / 26%

Middle East & Africa — 72% / 18%

Asia-Pacific — 38% / 44%

Source: Majority considers Internet access a human right (https://www.statista.com/chart/2991/internet-access-a-human-right/), Statista, 26 November 2014

earlier this month (November 2014). The United Nations has also been calling for the Internet to be considered a human right for over three years.

CIGI's research also found that over half (53%) of British Internet users are more concerned about online privacy today than they were one year ago – on both a private and public level.

Less than half (47%) said that government does a very good job of making sure the Internet is safe and secure, with only 28% of those surveyed believing that private information on the Internet is very secure.

Over two thirds are concerned about personal information being compromised, and three quarters are concerned about a criminal hacking into their personal bank accounts, while 70% are concerned about someone hacking into their online accounts and stealing personal information.

Meanwhile, 70% of Britons surveyed said they are concerned about institutions in their country being cyber-attacked by a foreign government or terrorist organisation, and around two-thirds are concerned about government agencies at home and abroad secretly monitoring their online activities.

"There is a gaping trust deficit in the Internet as people around the globe increasingly worry that their online identities and communications will be compromised or stolen by those who operate in the dark recesses of the Internet," said Hampson.

"Unless trust is restored in the Internet through creative governance innovations its real potential to promote human development and global prosperity will be severely compromised."

When given a choice of various governance sources for the Internet, the majority (57%) of those surveyed globally chose a multi-stakeholder model "of technology companies, engineers, non-governmental organisations and institutions that represent the interests and will of ordinary citizens, and governments".

Trust of multi-stakeholder governance of the Internet in Britain was lower than the average (53%), but it was still the most preferred ahead of options such as the United Nations. However, only 34% of Britons said they would trust their own government to play an important role in running the Internet.

25 November 2014

www.telegraph.co.uk

Mini glossary

Compromised – *if something has been compromised it has been weakened, damaged or put in danger.*

Deficit – *the loss or lack of something.*

Prosperity – *growth of good fortune, wealth and success.*

Stifle – *to smother and suppress (to hold back).*

Votes for prisoners: politics versus human rights law

By Conor James McKinney

> ➤ The European Court of Human Rights has repeatedly ruled that banning most prisoners from voting is a breach of their human rights.

> ➤ Although the UK has promised to abide by the Court's decisions, nobody can force Parliament to change the law on prisoner votes.

> ➤ The stalemate looks likely to continue for some time, but no compensation has ever been paid to a prisoner denied the vote.

The debate over votes for prisoners is perhaps the most politically controversial human rights question of them all. The European Court of Human Rights has now ruled on four occasions that the UK is violating prisoners' rights by banning almost all of them from voting. The UK has not yet changed the law in response to these judgements, which go back over a decade.

A long saga

In 2001, three prisoners challenged the explicit ban on all prisoners – except those on remand and a few other minor exceptions – being able to vote in any parliamentary or local government elections. They claimed that the ban was a breach of the European Convention on Human Rights, but lost in the High Court.

The UK has ratified the Convention, and made it a part of domestic law through the Human Rights Act 1998. Under the Convention, countries promise to hold elections "which will ensure the free expression of the opinion of the people".

One of the prisoners, John Hirst, convicted of manslaughter in 1980, argued at the human rights court in Strasbourg that this rules out a 'blanket' ban on prisoner votes. In 2005, the Court's Grand Chamber agreed that it was.

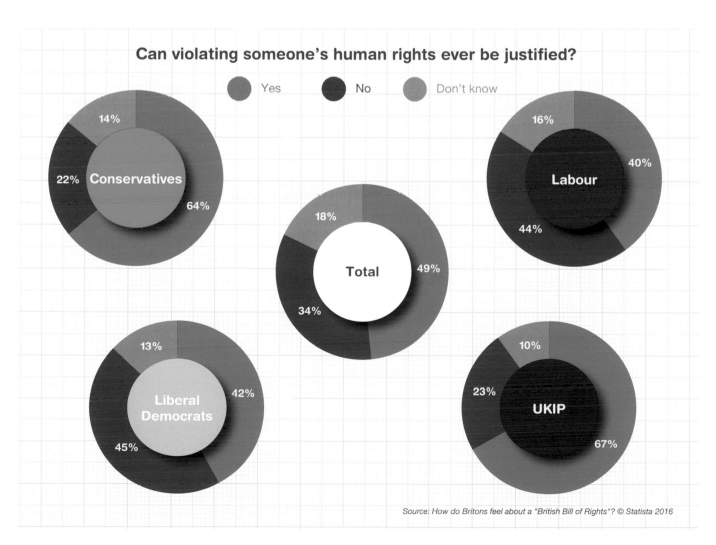

Can violating someone's human rights ever be justified?

Yes · No · Don't know

Conservatives: 14%, 22%, 64%

Labour: 16%, 40%, 44%

Total: 18%, 49%, 34%

Liberal Democrats: 13%, 42%, 45%

UKIP: 10%, 23%, 67%

Source: How do Britons feel about a "British Bill of Rights"? © Statista 2016

Prisoners have rights too

Its judgement said that nobody "forfeits his Convention rights merely because of his status as a person detained following conviction" and ruled out "automatic disenfranchisement based purely on what might offend public opinion". The Court felt that there hadn't been "any substantive debate by members of the legislature" on whether a ban on all convicted prisoners voting was a measured way of "preventing crime" and "enhancing civic responsibility and respect for the rule of law".

The Grand Chamber concluded that the law is disproportionate: "a blunt instrument".

It didn't say that *all* prisoners should have the vote. It's up to the UK to find a way of changing the law so that it's in keeping with what the Convention requires. This could be done by making the law more selective; for instance, giving some prisoners the vote, but not others, depending on the length of their sentence or the nature of their crime.

Politically toxic result

None of the three governments that have been in power since the ruling was made like it very much; but the UK has made a promise, in international law, to accept such judgements. Following the law means putting in place new legislation.

Different options for doing so have been discussed since 2005. In 2013, a parliamentary committee recommended that prisoners serving a sentence of 12 months or less should have the vote. The government responded in February 2014, saying that "the matter is under active consideration". The law went unchanged, perhaps due to the opposition of MPs and the general public.

Meanwhile, more prisoners have gone to the Strasbourg Court over the right to vote. A judgement in 2010 confirmed that the UK continues to be in breach of the Convention – but no action has been taken. A further ruling to that effect in 2014 denied the prisoners both compensation and the costs of taking the case. No financial compensation has ever been given to any prisoner who cannot vote.

Déjà vu

In its most recent ruling, made in February 2015, the Court found in favour of 1,015 prisoners or former prisoners – but once again refused to pay compensation or reimburse costs as a result.

The government said in December 2014 that it would not legislate for prisoners' votes in this Parliament, meaning that there will be no change to the law before the general election in May. The Council of Europe's Committee of Ministers, which has been urging the UK to honour its international law commitments, will next examine the government's progress in September 2015. The stalemate continues.

29 April 2016

www.fullfact.org

Mini glossary

Disenfranchisement – to take away a person's right of citizenship, such as the right to vote.

Reiterate – to give formal consent (like an agreement or contract).

Stalemate – there is no winner, things are at a standstill.

Qatar 2022 World Cup: Amnesty criticises FIFA over 'appalling' abuse of migrant workers

By Paul Wright

FIFA has been accused of failing to prevent systemic and "appalling" treatment of migrant workers helping to build and renovate stadiums for the 2022 World Cup in Qatar. A damning 50-page report by Amnesty International says that construction staff working on the Khalifa International Stadium in Doha lived in terrible conditions, are unpaid for months on end and have their passports taken away.

Qatar

Capital: Doha
Population: 2.5 million
Main language: Arabic
Major religion: Islam
Currency: Riyal

Amnesty also said it had uncovered evidence that the staff of one labour supply company used threats to force migrants to work including withholding pay, handing workers over to the police or stopping them from leaving Qatar. The human-rights organisation said this amounted to "forced labour" under international law.

The findings are based on interviews with 132 migrant workers involved in rebuilding the Khalifa Stadium – set to host one of the semi-finals in 2022 – and with a further 99 migrants helping landscape green spaces surrounding the Aspire Zone sporting complex, where Bayern Munich, Everton and Paris Saint-Germain trained during the last winter.

All those interviewed, mostly from Bangladesh, India and Nepal, reported abuse of one kind or another. All but six complained they had been lied to about what their job and pay would be before arriving. Migrant workers were also threatened for complaining about their conditions.

Salil Shetty, Amnesty's secretary general, called on Gianni Infantino, the new FIFA president and the governing body's sponsors, to take action.

"The abuse of migrant workers is a stain on the conscience of world football," Shetty said. "For players and fans, a World Cup stadium is a place of dreams. For some of the workers who spoke to us, it can feel like a living nightmare.

"Despite five years of promises, FIFA has failed almost completely to stop the World Cup being built on human-rights abuses. Indebted, living in squalid camps in the desert, paid a pittance, the lot of migrant workers contrasts sharply to that of the top-flight footballers who will play in the stadium. All workers want are their rights: to be paid on time, leave the country if need be and be treated with dignity and respect."

Amnesty said Qatar's kafala sponsorship system, under which migrant workers cannot change jobs or leave the country without their employer's permission, has been a big problem despite promises of change in late 2015. Some Nepali workers told Amnesty they were not even allowed to visit their loved ones after last year's earthquake that devastated their country.

Nabeel (name changed to protect identity), a metal worker from India who worked on the Khalifa stadium refurbishment, complained when he was not paid for several months but only received threats from his employer. "He just shouted abuse at me and said that if I complained again I'd never leave the country," he said. "Ever since I have been careful not to complain about my salary or anything else. Of course, if I could I would change jobs or leave Qatar."

Deepak (name changed to protect identity), a metal worker from Nepal, added: "My life here is like a prison. The work is difficult, we worked for many hours in the hot sun. When I first complained about my situation, soon after arriving in Qatar, the manager said 'if you [want to] complain you can but there will be consequences. If you want to stay in Qatar be quiet and keep working'."

This is the second report by Amnesty concerning the abuse of migrants working on Qatar's World Cup stadiums in less than four months. In December 2015, the organisation revealed similar findings following interviews with more than 400 migrant workers.

The latest allegations will yet again damage the reputation of Qatar's Supreme Committee for Delivery and Legacy, the organisation responsible for delivering the World Cup and which promised minimum standards would be met on the construction of stadiums. The number of people working on World Cup sites is set to surge almost tenfold to around 36,000 in the next two years.

Amnesty International is calling on major World Cup sponsors such as Adidas, Coca-Cola and McDonald's to pressure FIFA to address the exploitation of workers on the Khalifa Stadium, and disclose its plan for preventing further abuses in World Cup projects.

Qatar's Supreme Committee accused Amnesty of painting a "misleading" picture. It said its report was limited to just four companies out of more than 40

currently engaged on the Khalifa Stadium, and that the allegations dated back to early 2015. Since then, it said three companies had been banned from World Cup projects until they make improvements, while another had undergone "a comprehensive rectification process".

"The conditions reported were not representative of the whole work force," said the Qatar statement. "We wholly reject any notion that Qatar is unfit to host the World Cup."

A statement published by FIFA also disagreed with the findings. Federico Addiechi, FIFA's head of sustainability, said: "We closely monitor developments and address issues through our regular contact with the Supreme Committee.

"We have also met with a number of key stakeholders to discuss the best way forward. Of course many challenges remain, but we are on the right track and committed to continue improving, to further contribute to the protection of workers' rights at the FIFA World Cup stadium projects."

31 March 2016

Article original published at: http://www.ibtimes.co.uk/qatar-2022-world-cup-amnesty-criticises-fifa-over-appalling-abuse-migrant-workers-1552395

www.ibtimes.co.uk

Mini glossary

Allegations – *a claim, an accusation.*

Pittance – *a very small amount of money.*

Rectification – *to rectify something means to fix/correct it.*

Squalid – *horrible, poor, broken down.*

Why teach equality and human rights?

Why is it important to learn about equality and human rights?

Young people need to understand equality and know their rights, to understand both how they should be treated, and how they should treat others. Teaching these topics creates a safe place for students to explore, discuss, challenge and form their own opinions and values.

The knowledge and respect of rights that students gain from this, combined with understanding, respect and tolerance for difference, can empower them to tackle prejudice, improve relationships and make the most of their lives. In our ever more diverse and challenging society, it becomes more important to instil young people with these positive and open-minded attitudes.

What are the benefits of teaching these topics?

Educating students about equality and human rights empowers your students with learning they can use far beyond the classroom – in fact they will take it out into the school corridors and playground, into their homes and beyond into the wider community. The respect and tolerance it teaches will help students to create a healthier, happier, fairer school culture, and could lead to reductions in bullying and other negative behaviour, and improvements in attainment and aspirations. These are all essential outcomes that support the Government and Ofsted's strong focus on improving pupil behaviour and safety, tackling bullying and helping pupils achieve.

How do these topics fit into the curriculum?

As the curriculum changes, equality and human rights education's place may change. However, the topics naturally lend themselves to Citizenship and PSHE learning, and also allow you to bring core subjects to life, such as History, RE, English, Geography, Art and more. Teachers across all subjects could use the materials to confidently deliver lessons on equality and human rights through tutorials and assemblies.

An equality and human rights education is an essential part of high quality teaching and learning. The topical and real-life nature of the subjects can help schools to deliver a balanced, relevant curriculum that helps students to make sense of the wider world.

Why is it important to adopt a whole-school approach to equality and human rights?

To reap the full benefits of equality and human rights education, it is essential to teach the topics in an environment which respects the rights and differences of both students and teachers. Without an equality and human rights culture within the classroom and school as a whole, learning about these topics can at best appear irrelevant, and at worst, hypocritical.

How does teaching these topics support a teacher's legal duties?

Teaching equality and human rights helps schools and teachers to deliver their legal duties under the Equality Act 2010 and Human Rights Act 1998. Under the Equality Act 2010, maintained schools and academies, including free schools, must have due regard to the public sector equality duty (PSED). This means that they must take active steps to identify and address issues of discrimination where there is evidence of prejudice, harassment or victimisation, lack of understanding, disadvantage or lack of participation for individuals with protected characteristics (these being disability, gender reassignment, pregnancy and maternity, race, religion or belief, sex and sexual orientation). Under the Human Rights Act 1998, schools also have a legal duty to not act in a way that is incompatible with the European Convention on Human Rights. By developing students' understanding of equality and human rights, this can help to tackle prejudicial and harmful behaviour, help fufil to deliver your legal duties.

Disclaimer: This text is adapted from the original source which can be found at: https://www.equalityhumanrights. com/en/secondary-education-resources/useful-information/ why-teach-equality-and-human-rights.

www.equalityhumanrights.com

Pupils lack human rights understanding as a third of teachers feel ill-equipped to teach it, says new poll

By Michael Grimes

A poll commissioned by Amnesty International and teachers' magazine TES has found that one in three teachers (32.9 per cent) do not feel equipped to teach human rights. Nearly half (47.4 per cent) think their pupils do not understand the concept of human rights.

The survey also found that 46 per cent of children are unaware of their own human rights.

"One in three teachers (32.9 per cent) do not feel equipped to teach human rights."

The TES-Amnesty survey was commissioned ahead of Amnesty's Youth Awards, to assess how well human rights is understood in British schools and the level of commitment to it. It reveals a patchy level of confidence in teaching human rights and a varied degree of knowledge among students.

These findings are concerning but hardly surprising. Although 'human rights' is on the statutory citizenship curriculum, it is only explicit at key stage 4; key stage 3 requires students to learn about 'precious liberties' but not 'human rights'. On top of that, about half of schools – that is, free schools and academies – are exempt from teaching the citizenship curriculum; and primary schools don't have one to teach in the first place.

"Nearly half [of teachers surveyed (47.4 per cent) think their pupils do not understand the concept of human rights."

Ann Mroz, Editor of TES, said:

"At a time of heightened interest in human rights it is fascinating that teachers feel there is much work to be done in this area in schools and in curriculum terms. As we look towards the anniversary of Magna Carta this year, it is surely good news that teachers believe teaching human rights is so important."

Amnesty International's Youth Awards Project Manager, Alice Edwards, said:

"These findings are a concern. Imagine if we were talking about English, Maths or Science? Human Rights are principles upon which we rely on a daily basis. But at Amnesty we know it's not always easy for teachers to find the space for human rights education in schools. That's why we do everything we can to produce relevant, enriching curriculum linked resources to support teachers in engaging their students."

Amnesty International spoke to a few of its student members to ask whether they agreed with these findings and what their peers thought of human rights.

"46 per cent of children are unaware of their own human rights."

Seventeen-year-old Rona Hardie said:

"Unfortunately there is a stigma that surrounds standing up for human rights amongst most teenagers I know. But on the other hand there is a basic understanding of what it means to have a human right and why it is important."

Lizzie Wood, also 17, of Berkhamsted School, added:

"The idea of 'human rights' is thrown about a lot, but not many question what it actually means. To many, it is a convenient excuse. People know they have rights, but not what exactly they are, or what impact not having rights would have.

"In a society, and in a privileged corner of England, human rights are not discussed because they are never truly denied. When not personally affected, I find that global issues only go skin deep. Human rights are not a problem for the lucky few and therefore unworthy of attention. Like so many other commodities, we have taken them for granted."

16 January 2015

www.democraticlife.org.uk

Activities

Brainstorm

1.	Why is it important to learn about equality and human rights?

Oral activities

2.	Three quarters of Britons consider Internet access a 'human right'. Do you agree or disagree? Why? Discuss in groups and feedback to the class.

3.	Which human rights matter most? Make a list of your top five most important rights that matter to you. Compare your list with a partner and discuss the reasoning behind your choices. How did your lists differ? How were they similar?

Research activity

4.	The debate over votes for prisoners is perhaps the most politically controversial human rights question of them all. Research into this issue and present your findings and opinions on the matter. You might find *Votes for prisoners: politics versus human rights law* on page 21 helpful.

Written activity

5.	Read *Qatar 2022 World Cup: Amnesty criticises FIFA over 'appalling' abuse of migrant workers* on page 23. Imagine that you are one of the workers in Qatar. Write a diary entry describing the conditions and your experiences. You may want to do a bit more research on the situation beforehand.

Moral dilemma

6.	Can violating someone's human rights ever be justified? Discuss this statement as a class.

Design activities

7.	Prepare a lesson plan for younger students to teach them what human rights are and why they are important. You can create a PowerPoint, handouts, a video or even a skit to help get your teachings across.

8.	Create an informative poster about child marriage to help promote awareness of this issue. You might want to include some informative statistics.

Key facts

- Human rights are universal. They apply to all people simply on the basis of being human. (page 1)

- Human rights cannot be taken away from someone. They can only be limited in certain tightly-defined circumstances and some rights, such as the prohibition on torture and slavery, can never be limited. (page 1)

- In 1998 the Human Rights Act was passed, making the rights and freedoms in the European Convention on Human Rights directly enforceable in the UK. It entered into force on 2 October 2000. (page 1)

- In 1948, in the aftermath of the Second World War, the newly formed United Nations adopted the Universal Declaration of Human Rights (UDHR). (page 1)

- The European Court of Human Rights was established in 1959 and the United Kingdom has allowed an individual right of application to the Court since 1966. (page 2)

- About a quarter of the victims referred to the UK Human Trafficking Centre are children. (page 4)

- Whilst people smuggling always involves illegal border crossing and entry into another country, human trafficking for exploitation can happen within someone's own country, including Britain. (page 5)

- When surveyed, in Britain, USA, Germany, France, Denmark, Sweden, Finland and Norway more than 50% of respondents selected free speech as one of the most important rights. It is the only right to which this applies. (page 15)

- Far more Americans than Europeans value the right to own a gun (selected by 46% of Americans, but by no more than 6% in any European country). (page 16)

- Each year, 15 million girls are married before the age of 18. That is 28 girls every minute. (page 17)

- If there is no reduction in child marriage, an additional 1.2 billion girls will be married by 2050. (page 17)

- In 2001, three prisoners challenged the explicit ban on all prisoners – except those on remand and a few other minor exceptions – being able to vote in any parliamentary or local government elections. They claimed that the ban was a breach of the European Convention on Human Rights, but lost in the High Court. (page 21)

- Teaching equality and human rights helps schools and teachers to deliver their legal duties under the Equality Act 2010 and Human Rights Act 1998. (page 25)

- A poll commissioned by Amnesty International and teachers' magazine TES has found that one in three teachers (32.9 per cent) do not feel equipped to teach human rights. The survey also found that 46 per cent of children are unaware of their own human rights. (page 26)

Glossary

Child marriage – Where children, often before they have reached puberty, are given to be married – often to a person many years older.

Domestic servitude – A type of labour trafficking. Domestic workers perform household tasks such as child-care, cleaning, laundry and cooking.

European Convention on Human Rights – The European Convention on Human Rights was adopted by the Council of Europe in 1950 to enshrine the articles of the Universal Declaration of Human Rights, a declaration drafted in the aftermath of the Second World War in response to the horrors of the Holocaust. The UK signed up to the Convention in 1951.

Female genital mutilation (FGM) – FGM is a non-medical cultural practice that involves partially or totally removing a girl or woman's external genitalia.

Forced labour – When someone is forced to work, or provide services, against their will. This is often the result of a person being trafficked into another country and then having their passport withheld, or threats made against their family.

Forced marriage – A marriage that takes place without the consent of one or both parties. Forced marriage is not the same as arranged marriage, which is organised by family or friends but which both parties freely enter into.

Human rights – The basic rights all human beings are entitled to, regardless of who they are, where they live or what they do. Concepts of human rights have been present throughout history, but our modern understanding of the term emerged as a response to the horrific events of the Holocaust.

Human trafficking – The transport and/or trade of people from one area to another, usually for the purpose of forcing them into labour or prostitution.

Millennium Development Goals (MDG) – In 2000, agreed upon by 193 United Nations member states, the Millennium Development Goals are the world's targets for addressing poverty, education, disease, equality and environmental sustainability (made up of eight goals). The aim was to achieve these goals by the year 2015. From 2016 onwards, the Sustainable Development Goals (SDGs) have replaced the MDGs.

Slavery – A slave is someone who is denied their freedom, forced to work without pay and considered to be literally someone else's property. Although slavery is officially banned internationally, there are an estimated 27 million slaves worldwide.

The Human Rights Act – The Human Rights Act is a written law (statute) passed in 1998 which is in force in England and Wales. The rights that are protected by this law are based on the articles of the European Convention on Human Rights. There is an ongoing debate between supporters of the Act and its critics as to whether it should be kept, or replaced with a new UK Bill of Rights.

Torture – Intentionally causing a person physical or mental pain or suffering in order to obtain information or force them to make a confession.

United Nations Convention on the Rights of the Child (UNCRC) – An international human rights treaty that protects the rights of all children and young people under 18. The UK signed the convention on 19 April 1990 and ratified it on 16 December 1991. When a country ratifies the convention it agrees to do everything it can to implement it. Every country in the world has signed the convention except the USA and Somalia.

Universal Declaration of Human Rights – The first international agreement on what were formerly called 'the rights of man'. After the traumas of the Second World War, in order to prevent something similar happening again, the world's governments set out a shared bill of rights for all peoples and all nations. The text is non-binding, but it retains its force as the primary authority on human rights.